AF270590

LOS ANGELES CHARGERS

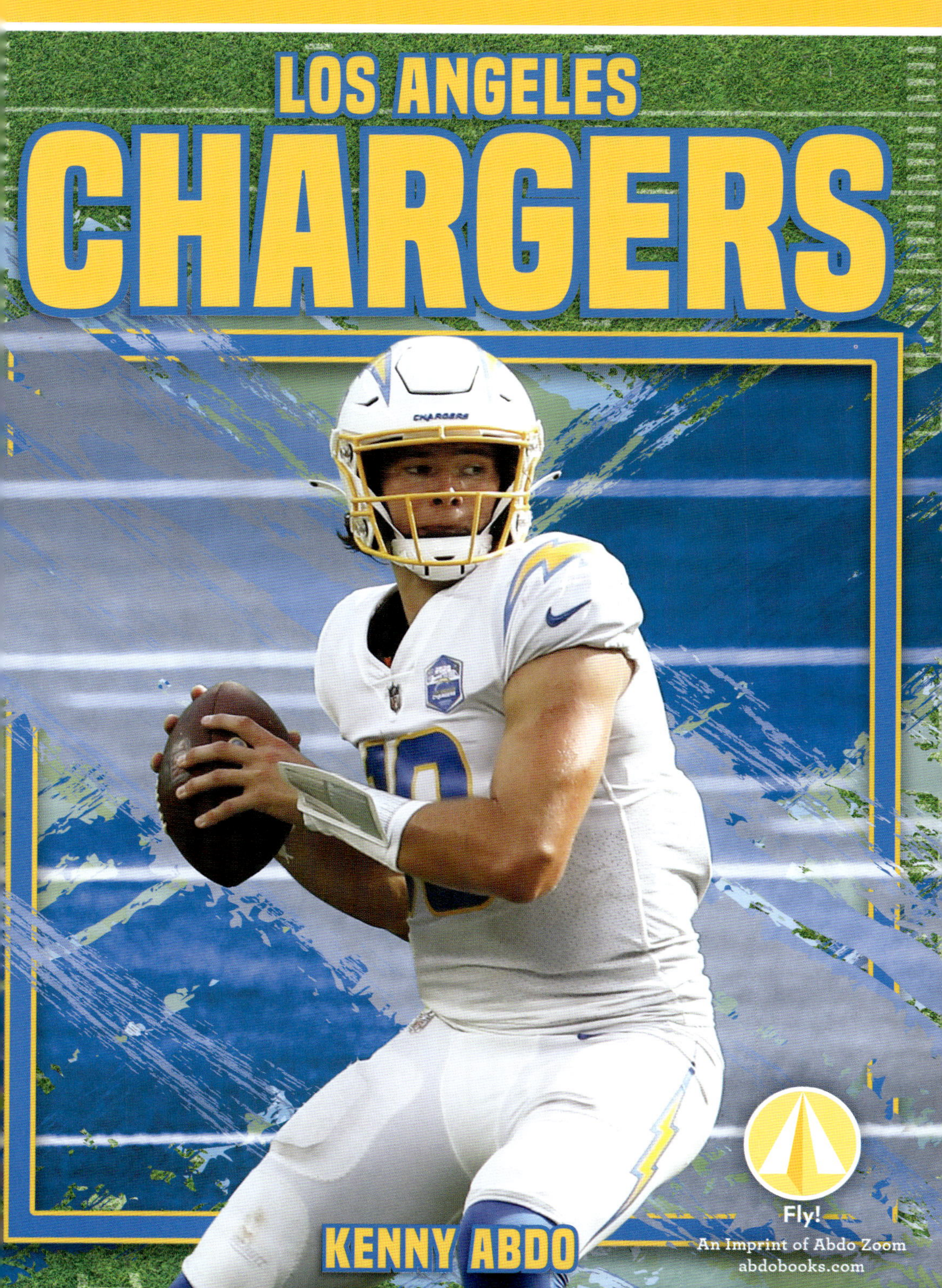

KENNY ABDO

abdobooks.com

Published by Abdo Zoom, a division of ABDO, P.O. Box 398166, Minneapolis, Minnesota 55439. Copyright © 2022 by Abdo Consulting Group, Inc. International copyrights reserved in all countries. No part of this book may be reproduced in any form without written permission from the publisher. Fly!™ is a trademark and logo of Abdo Zoom.

Printed in China.
052021
092021

Photo Credits: Alamy, AP Images, iStock, Shutterstock PREMIER
Production Contributors: Kenny Abdo, Jennie Forsberg, Grace Hansen
Design Contributors: Candice Keimig, Neil Klinepier

Library of Congress Control Number: 2020919729

Publisher's Cataloging-in-Publication Data

Names: Abdo, Kenny, author.
Title: Los Angeles Chargers / by Kenny Abdo
Description: Minneapolis, Minnesota : Abdo Zoom, 2022 | Series: NFL teams | Includes online resources and index.
Identifiers: ISBN 9781098224684 (lib. bdg.) | ISBN 9781098225629 (ebook) | ISBN 9781098226091 (Read-to-Me ebook)
Subjects: LCSH: Los Angeles Chargers (Football team)--Juvenile literature. | National Football League--Juvenile literature. | Football teams--Juvenile literature. | American football--Juvenile literature. | Professional sports--Juvenile literature.
Classification: DDC 796.33264--dc23

TABLE OF CONTENTS

LOS ANGELES CHARGERS

Taking charge of the ball, the Los Angeles Chargers are electrifying on the field!

CHARGERS
82
CHARGERS
24
MATHEWS
TOYOTA
GEICO
GARY JOHNSON   63 DOUG WILKERSON

Throughout their decades of play, the Chargers have always managed to bring a spark of excitement to the sport.

KICK OFF

Businessman Barron Hilton founded the Chargers in 1959. Based out of Los Angeles, California, the team played their first game in 1960, beating the Dallas Texans by just one point!

After one year in Los Angeles, the Chargers moved to San Diego. They beat the Oakland Raiders in their first regular season home game in their new city.

The Chargers won 12 of 14 games in the 1961 season. They lost the **championship** game to the Oilers 10-3. Two years later, the Chargers won the 1963 AFL Game against the Boston Patriots 51-10!

56
20

TEAM RECAPS

Rolf Benirschke kicked an amazing 29-yard field goal with just 45 seconds left in a 1981 playoff game. The Chargers beat the Dolphins 41-38 in **overtime**. The game was so thrilling, it was later called the "Epic in Miami."

The Chargers won their **division**, beating the Miami Dolphins in the 1994 playoffs. They also beat the Steelers in the **AFC championship**. The team lost **Super Bowl** XXIX to the 49ers 49–26.

In 2017, the Chargers moved back to Los Angeles. They ended the 2018 season with a 12-4 record, making it to their first playoff in five years.

The Chargers beat the Ravens 23–17 at the 2018 **AFC** Wild Card game. They lost their next playoff game to the Patriots. The Chargers had a disappointing 2019 season with a 5–11 record.

The 2020 season brought a new stadium with it. SoFi Stadium was completed in July and ready to host the Chargers' home games.

It was also the team's first season without **QB** Philip Rivers since 2004. The Chargers ended the season with a 7–9 record.

HALL OF FAME

Tight end Kellen Winslow had 6,741 receiving yards and 45 touchdowns in his nine seasons. He caught 13 passes in the 1981 playoffs beating the Dolphins. Winslow played so hard in that game, he had to be helped off the field by his teammates.

Winslow was **inducted** into the Pro Football Hall of Fame in 1995.

Antonio Gates, another tight end, is the all-time leader in receptions, receiving yards, and touchdown catches for the Chargers. His teammates voted him the Offensive Player of the Year four times. Gates was chosen to play in the Pro Bowl eight times.

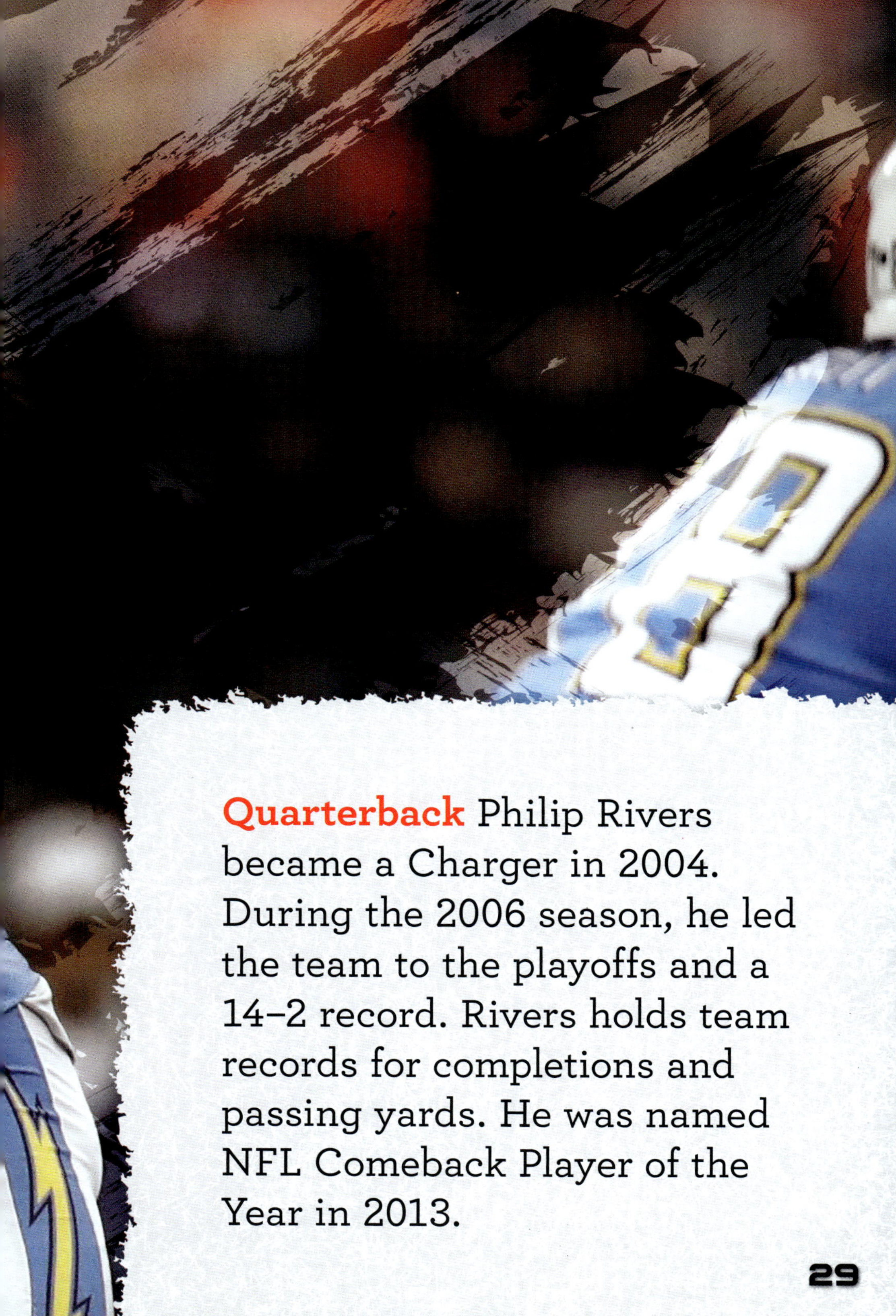

Quarterback Philip Rivers became a Charger in 2004. During the 2006 season, he led the team to the playoffs and a 14–2 record. Rivers holds team records for completions and passing yards. He was named NFL Comeback Player of the Year in 2013.

GLOSSARY

American Football Conference (AFC) – one of two major conferences of the NFL. Each conference contains 16 teams split into four divisions. The winner of the AFC championship plays the NFC winner at the Super Bowl.

championship – a game held to find a first-place winner.

division – a group of teams who compete against each other for a championship.

induct – to admit someone as a member of an organization.

overtime – additional minutes added to a tied-up game giving each team a chance to win.

quarterback (QB) – the player on the offensive team that directs teammates in their play.

Super Bowl – the NFL championship game, played once a year.

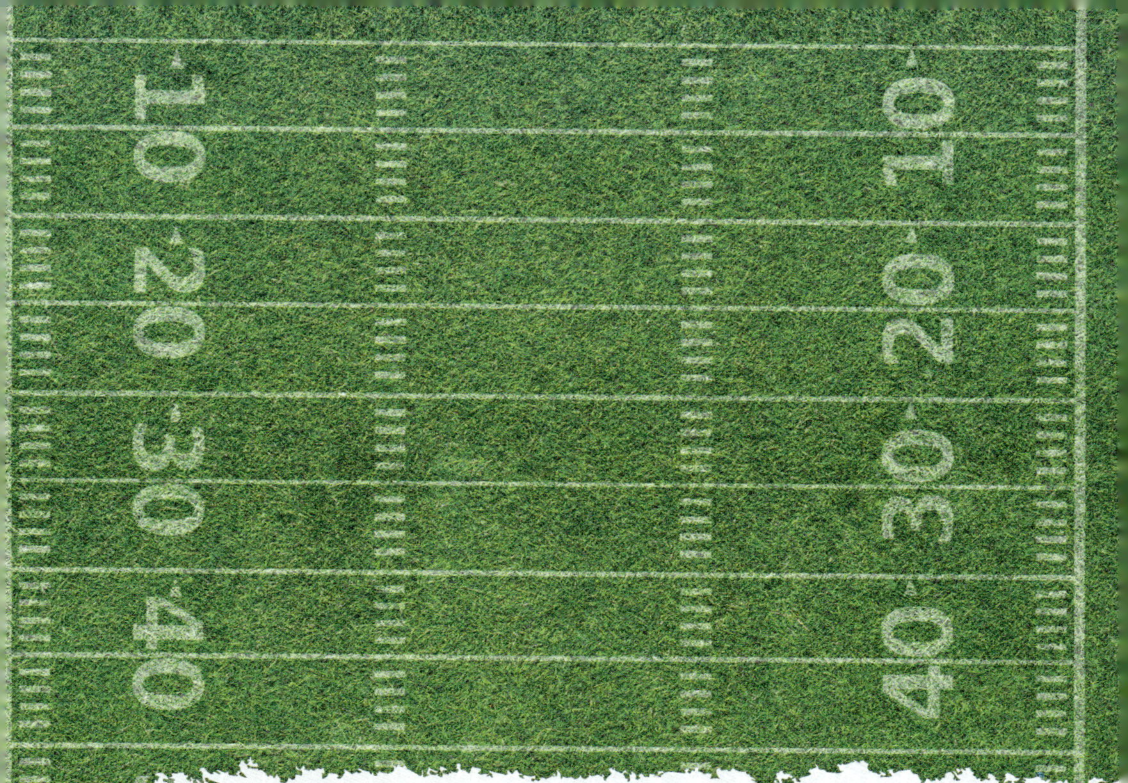

ONLINE RESOURCES

To learn more about the Los Angeles Chargers, please visit abdobooklinks.com or scan this QR code. These links are routinely monitored and updated to provide the most current information available.

INDEX